Death Smiles at All of Us

CHILD DEATH IN VICTORIAN SCOTLAND

KAYDEN ABLEY

DEATH SMILES AT ALL OF US

CONTENTS

DEDICATION

To my beloved city, Edinburgh, and to all of its children and families, past and present. To every person suffering with grief and loss.

-K.A.

ACKNOWLEDGEMENTS

To Professor Ewen Cameron and Professor Louise Jackson at the University of Edinburgh, without whom this short book would not have been written - your insight and expertise during my time writing my MSc. thesis at the University of Edinburgh helped me get through one of the toughest periods of my life, and your insights and feedback helped me get through my MSc. thesis.

To my parents, Ann Beer (PhD, McGill University) and Mark Abley (PhD, University of Saskatoon), who proofread the early versions of this - I am indebted to your editing skills (and support of me, as your eldest child).

To my spouse, Max Nardella, who encouraged me every step of the way in turning this half-finished manuscript into a short book that I am proud of - thank you for your everlasting support, love, affection, laughter, and walks. Thank you for making sure I ate food when all I wanted was to scribble away, writing for hours on end. You have made my life what it is today.

1

INTRODUCTION

People often try to make sense of what they do not, or cannot, understand, and one subject that intrigues and terrifies us most is death. While dying is an experience that everyone must go through, many do not know how to react to the thought of their own eventual demise, and some find it even harder to imagine the deaths of their loved ones. Humans often embrace optimism, preferring to focus on what they can control, as opposed to what they cannot, and death is perhaps the most uncertain part of life. We cannot know exactly what happens after we die, and some individuals prefer to ignore the fact that death is a part of human existence, living their lives as best they can, while others might choose to focus on mortality, working in such careers as funeral directors, grief counsellors, or forensic pathologists.

One country that people associate with death is Scotland, in the United Kingdom (also known as "the UK"). Scotland is the country that grave robbers (and eventual serial killers) Burke and Hare operated in as a duo, when they were desperate for money and realized that the best way to get it involved providing the University of Edinburgh's anatomy department with fresh bodies (no matter how the corpses were obtained, leading to their grave-robbing becoming the more lucrative practice of serial killing). In modern times, Scotland inspired the darkness of the many deaths in J. K. Rowling's Harry Potter series, along with countless murder mysteries, films, and television series. One of Shakespeare's most famous, or infamous, plays is *Macbeth*, also known as "The Scottish Play," as many Shakespearean actors believe that even saying the name "Macbeth" in a theater will cause bad luck (injuries, disasters, etc.).

When I did my MSc. thesis at the University of Edinburgh in Scottish Studies, I marveled at Scottish funerals, where funeral directors would drive carriages carrying coffins, led by teams of two to four horses, and both the horses and the funeral directors would be dressed in Victorian-style outfits. At times, I wondered if I was hallucinating (then I looked up funeral websites, discovering that people had the option of paying for Victorian-style funerals, complete with horses wearing large plumed feathers in their bridles, funeral directors wearing top hats, old-fashioned suits, and carrying whips – an option that certainly did not exist in suburban Canada, where I was from). It was surreal to watch such a funeral procession march down the cobbled high street, slowing down impatient twenty-first century locals in cars and vans. While studying there, I actually lived in an apartment (a.k.a. a flat) above a funeral home. It certainly reminded me that death was never very far away. My fascination with death led me to writing my 2011 MSc. thesis at the University of Edinburgh on child death in nineteenth-century Scotland, a topic so under-researched at the time that various academics and archive/library staff tried to discourage me from doing it. Once the dissertation had been completed, and my MSc. granted, I couldn't forget about the topic, or the research I had done – and this led to the creation of this short book, written years later. I hope that you enjoy it. (It might be best to read this on a misty autumn night, wrapped up in a warm blanket, while drinking a cup of comforting hot chocolate or apple cider, while the wind

howls outside.)

2

"Pure Dead Brilliant!": Researching Folktales, Novels, and Newspaper Articles

Many scholars examining death and grief have discussed the topic of death using a historical viewpoint, while others have taken a more literary approach and examined novels, poems, and other fictional creative outlets. Others, more versed in science and technology than I am, have studied medical journals and statistics to examine precisely how and why certain children in Scotland died in the nineteenth century – of what diseases and under what circumstances. Sadly though, many scholars have looked at death as a whole, without taking into account different cultures, geographies, customs, and societal norms, including the class system, poverty, discrimination, marginalization, diets, etc. This made finding any data on Scotland-specific material incredibly challenging.

One valuable source on Scottish death literary and archival history is the National Museum of Scotland's 1996 publication *Scottish Endings: Writings on Death.* The book, compiled by Andrew Martin, discusses epitaphs, poems, folktales and photographs. While many of the epitaphs, photographs of memorial objects and records of everyday life of Scotland are fascinating, few of them have to do with child death, and many are outside this book's preferred time period, i.e. they are from either the eighteenth century or twentieth century (Martin 76-77). Two proverbs, quoted in Martin's work, which are applicable to child death in Scotland are: "Oor first breath is the beginning o daith," signifying that as soon as one is born, one is destined to die; and "Death is deaf, an will hear nae denial," meaning that even if one does not wish to die, one has no choice, and similarly, though a nineteenth-century parent would not have wanted their child to die, they would have been pressured accept it by the norms and standards of the society in which they lived (Martin 12). While such statements can be considered bleak and grim, reflecting on death allows us to also appreciate life, while we are still fortunate enough to be alive.

People have always had to cope with death, and many did, and continue to do so, with rituals - including funeral rites. Peter C. Jupp and Glennys Howarth co-edited the work *The Changing Face of Death: Historical Accounts of Death and Disposal*, a fascinating work whose essays examine the many ways in which people grieve and react to death. When one thinks of death, one rarely imagines the funeral trade itself, and yet meaningful funeral ceremonies and funerary rites, even healing from grief, depend on it, to an extent. Julian Litten's essay "The Funeral Trade in Hanoverian England 1714-1760" reminds us that "undertaking had become a necessary, rather than a popular, trade" as it was something that the public needed, but "few undertakers expected, or got, much thanks for their pains" (Litten 59). Similarly, Clare Gittings' essay "Expressions of Loss in Seventeenth Century England," though it is centered on a time period earlier than the one I am examining for this book, makes some intriguing points about personal loss, the writing on tombstones and when it became commonly accepted for individuals to grieve openly for their loved ones. Gittings comments that such a change is at "a societal level [...] but leads to the commemoration of the dead with greater individuality" (Gittings 28).

While this statement may be applicable to English tombstones from the seventeenth century onwards, it certainly does not appear to have been the norm for Scottish children's tombstones in the nineteenth century. The majority of nineteenth-century tombstones with children's names on them in both the Greyfriars churchyard and the Canongate Kirk in Edinburgh, Scotland, merely give the child's name, age, and the date they died, and some do not even provide that. That is in startling contrast to the adults' tombstones from the same time period, which are often covered with sentimental verses and quotes from the Bible. Having explored both graveyards, I was able to find only a couple of exceptions. An example of this was the inscription on a tombstone in Greyfriars churchyard of a girl named Agnes Muschett, who was the fifth daughter in her family, and who died on July 9, 1813, at the age of nine. She, unlike most Scottish children who died during the nineteenth century, has an epitaph, stating, "Out of the mouths of babes and sucklings / Thou hast perfected praise." This makes one wonder why children's tombstones in nineteenth century Scotland were so often denied the same amount of sentiment and public grieving as those of adults. It is also in contrast to places like Pere Lachaise cemetery in France, which has dozens, if not hundreds, of elaborately-decorated children's gravestones adorned with angels, cherubs, doves, child figures, etc.

Perhaps it was because the grief felt by nineteenth-century Scottish adults over the deaths of children tended to be expressed more privately, despite being deeply felt, as was the cultural norm at the time, or, more likely, that many poorer parents could not afford elaborate tombstones. People today in 2023 still have to make devastating choices about how to grieve lost children; do they spend thousands on an elaborate funeral? If they choose not to use what money they have for that purpose, will they be seen by others as miserly and uncaring? Some would argue yes; others would argue no. Having spent time as a student studying to be a funeral director in Canada, I can attest that even funeral directors feel divided and conflicted on the "correct" ways to hold a funeral ceremony, and how much grieving families should pay for a service. There are no easy answers when it comes to planning any funeral service, let alone one for a child. I had three classmates who ended up becoming funeral directors as a way to give back to the deathcare community, after having had their own child(ren) die, but many people would not choose this career path, as it would remind them daily what they had lost.

How do people even begin to understand death? How did views on death change over time? Andrew Martin's book *Scottish Endings: Writings on Death* recounts an incident, discussed in a newspaper article, that happened in Edinburgh, where in June 1936, a group of boys stumbled upon a collection of tiny coffins, hidden in part of a large hill named Arthur's Seat, in Edinburgh. (This peak used to be a volcano, once upon a time, which now lies dormant and is often explored by locals and tourists.) The boys, searching for rabbit burrows, stumbled upon a tiny opening in one of the rocks which looked like it had pieces of slate in front to protect the inside of the hole, and when the boys explored further, they found "seventeen Lilliput-ian coffins" inside (Martin 42). The coffins all contained miniature figures made out of wood, carved like human people and dressed in decaying scraps of clothing (Martin 42-43). While such figures and their coffins are mysterious, and provide insight into rituals surrounding death, the story also reminds us of how many celebrate life more than revering death, as the following example demonstrates. After the boys' discovery of the tiny coffins, they then acci-dentally destroyed some of them by "pelting them at each other as unmeaning and contemptible trifles" (Martin 43). Such an action shows that they might have valued play and frivolity over death, loss, or historical artifacts.

There are many books written on death and grief, often touching such topics as mourning and poverty, but they focus on Britain as a whole, never differentiating between England, Wales, or Scotland. Anne Gordon's *Death is for the Living*, for example, covers many topics to do with nineteenth-century death, including the issue of unbap-tized children (Gordon 143-145). Gordon argues that, through no fault of their own, dead infants and still-born children were often discriminated against, owing to the strict laws surrounding proper burials in churchyards.

There were even designated areas for unbaptized children, but few records survive, and it is often very difficult to find specific sources for Scotland – I have only been able to find references that support scholars' views on Britain in general, or even just England. On the Scottish island of Iona, in the 1690s, unbaptized children were "buried along with murderers in a piece of empty ground between St Mary's Church and the gardens" (Gordon 144). Similarly, at "Watten in Caithness they were buried along with [beggars] on the site of a ruined chapel at Scouthal, while in the parish of Nigg, Ross and Cromarty," such unbaptized infants were laid to rest "around the ancient Pictish Shandwick Stone, along with suicides, until 1790" (Gordon 144). This demonstrates what the official Christian churches thought of unbaptized children, that because their souls would be unable to enter heaven, they were laid to rest beside murderers and suicides.

One issue that comes up now and again is the topic of silence around child death. Scholar Julie-Marie Strange's excellent book *Death, Grief and Poverty in Britain, 1870-1914* includes a chapter on grieving for dead children which shows how the high infant mortality rates, especially among the working class, often led to middle-class people and newspapers blaming working-class parents for neglect and brutality (Strange 230-231). This is a complex topic, for although some parents were indeed responsible for a child's death (either deliberately, by murdering them in a drunken rage, or accidentally, by the suffocation of young children sleeping in the same crowded bed as their parents), many more working-class parents loved their children desperately and wanted to do their best by them (Strange 247). Families often had no choice but to sleep close together – if families were unable to afford more than one bed or were sharing a single room, or even a corner of a room, together, they would have had no choice but to sleep in the same bed, risking potential harm to the children. Such living spaces would also have been very cold (even now, many UK families don't have, or can't afford, central heating) and many poorer nineteenth-century families would have preferred to conserve heat by sleeping close together.

Similar to the silence around the topic of child death on Scottish children's gravestones, many working-class parents were silent after their children's deaths, but this seems to have often been misunderstood by those around them. Some wealthier people saw the "expressions of resignation," and did not stop to think about the "self-sacrifice and solicitous care mothers typically exercised towards their children," and casual observers often viewed the "apparent composure of parents [...] as evidence of apathy" towards their child's death (Strange 254). More can be read into this though, as often the working class's "linguistic inarticulacy often reflected the incoherence, incomprehension and frustration of grief" (Strange 254). Therefore silence around the topic of child death in Britain did not mean that parents did not feel grief or sorrow. While people might not have discussed their grief aloud, especially with strangers, that did not mean that they were not fighting private inner battles of sorrow, turmoil, anger, denial, grief, and other emotions. Families who were struggling to survive, striving to find and keep jobs, to put food on the table, could not afford to risk breaking down with grief -they had to keep going if they were to keep themselves, and their other loved ones, alive. As a working administrative professional, working full-time in 2023, who has had to use food banks to survive and help keep my household afloat due to inflation and the rising costs of living, I understand these nineteenth-century adults' struggles a great deal more now than I did when I first started researching and writing about child death in Scotland (in 2011).

Sorche Nic Leodhas 's intriguing collection of Scottish folk tales, *Thistle and Thyme: Tales and Legends from Scotland*, draws its sources from oral sources, handed down over generations, thus making it impossible to attach accurate dates to the original tales. Nic Leodhas' work covers aspects of Scottish folklore with more literary skill than in many of the nineteenth-century collectors' versions. A case in point is her tale "The Changeling and the Fond Young Mother," which from its title hints at the story's plot: that the young mother's human infant can be swapped for a fairy changeling as a form of punishment for the over-proud and boastful mother. The tale also acts as a warning to others to be humble. Nic Leodhas' work, while written in English, has retained many of its Gaelic origins, in terms of pronunciation and names, and the compilation is also valuable as it informs its reader which part(s) of Scotland the tale originates from.

Another twentieth-century book of tales, Barbara Ker Wilson's *Scottish Folktales and Legends*, while not as helpful on the topic of childhood death as nineteenth-century authors Lord Archibald Campbell, Robert Chambers, Elizabeth Grierson and the twentieth-century Nic Leodhas, does include some references to Scottish people's fears of changelings, and consequently child death (Ker Wilson 69). For example, "The Faery Flag of Dunvegan" hints at how worried people were over child death, as the tale concerns a happy marriage between a king and a fairy woman, but when she tires of the human realms, she leaves her child behind with its human father (Ker Wilson 66-67). Though the castle's inhabitants know of the fairy woman who married their king, and thus know the fairies' capacity for kindness and love, they still worry about the child at all times, fearing it will one day be replaced with a changeling (Ker Wilson 69). This shows just how scared people were over the prospect of child death, of something that could take a child away forever. Many of Nic Leodhas' and Ker Wilson's tales do not discuss child death directly, but contain vague references to it that must be searched for. This appears to be characteristic of all Scottish folktales, whether they were written down in the nineteenth century or the twentieth. Such caution implies that people were so afraid of the potential consequences of discussing death openly that they only felt able to hint at it in tales and stories.

Gillian Avery and Kimberley Reynolds are the editors of one of the most relevant sources of scholarship on the topic of child death in Britain, *Representations of Childhood Death*, and while there are many other valuable essays, books and collections of primary oral sources, all discussing the topic of child death in England, the same cannot be said of research on child death in Scotland in particular. The works that do mention Scottish sources have seldom taken into account that the source is Scottish, not English, and it seems odd that few have looked at this issue before. Among the sources for child death and death in Scotland, I am particularly indebted to Avery and Reynolds. Their introduction to *Representations of Childhood Death* provides a much-needed analysis of the topic in general, highlighting how the topic of adult death has been studied in great detail, but the topic of child death has not. Their compilation of essays examines historical aspects of child death, as well as accompanying representations in folklore, diaries, ballads, novels, songs, epitaphs, and other monuments to dead, or dying, children.

One chapter in their book, written by Jacqueline Simpson, entitled "The Folklore of Infant Deaths: Burials, Ghosts and Changelings," provided valuable insight and background information on the subject of child death and folklore, including medical explanations for so-called changelings. Another chapter which was integral to the topic of child death in literature was Kimberley Reynolds' "Fatal Fantasies: the Death of Children in Victorian and Edwardian Fantasy Writing." Reynolds discusses the reasons why child death was often presented as positive or desirable, as disturbing as that sounds to modern audiences. Some authors wanted to highlight deplorable domestic conditions and class differences, whereas others tried to give their reader a more positive view of death in order to make them less afraid of it. The nineteenth-century Scottish author George MacDonald occasionally brings up the former in his works, but focuses most of his attention on the latter; this will be discussed further in my later chapters.

Many of Avery and Reynolds' essays discuss how people often interpreted child death as a punishment - for the parents. The research suggests that in most cases, the Christian parents believed it to be God's vengeance due to their "neglecting their duties to Him, or for loving their children too much" (Avery and Reynolds 3). Avery and Reynolds state that "the frequency of such explanations could suggest that writers were simply conforming to or making use of established conventions," but other scholars believe that it was much more complicated than that (Avery and Reynolds 3). When one reads "private accounts such as letters and journals," one discovers how many parents – even "during times when religious faith and belief in the afterlife were generally unquestioned – [tried] to accept their loss," and understand and "reconcile themselves to God's anger in ways which are anything but clichéd or facile" (Avery and Reynolds 3). This statement holds true not just for English sources, but Scottish ones too, as in my chapter on biographical and autobiographical accounts, I discuss George MacDonald's grieving for his dead children through his personal letters and poems. It is remarkable that scholars, to date, have neglected Scottish archival sources for their research on death. Personal emails from English historian Clare Gittings enabled me to realize that if I wanted to pursue the topic, I would have to widen my search beyond archival sources and write using the material that was available. It is partly thanks to her advice that I found my sources in Scottish folktales, biographical and autobiographical details taken from both letters and journals, and secondary literature from biographers of author George MacDonald and young diarist Marjory Fleming, as well as MacDonald's literary works and nineteenth-century Scottish newspapers. I have tried to find more current anecdotes of scholarship around child death that are trauma-informed and based on disability advocacy, and update the manuscript text as needed. That said, many texts discuss disability and/or trauma, but not historical/literary child death, or vice-versa. I have done what I could to be as inclusive and aware as possible.

Adults today often try to conceal the reality of death from children, informing them that a deceased person is not dead, but merely sleeping, or away travelling, thinking that this will soften the blow to the child. Understandably, this leads to the child's retaining hope that the deceased will come back to life, and in a more personal way, come back to them somehow. Some children cling to such hopes, and find it harder to cope with their grief when they learn that their loved one will never return. In a more practical way, this can also cause problems for the child, if they begin associating sleep, or travelling, with a person dying, or being gone forever. While one might think that nineteenth-century children and adults were less troubled by death than people today, the fictional and "factual" pieces of the time, especially the literary works and life of author George MacDonald, as well as various folktales, and newspapers, collectively indicate that this was not the case.

MacDonald had very particular views on children and childhood, morality, and goodness. He stated that "everyone had to become like a little child before they could enter the Kingdom of Heaven, and so, though he found fame as a children's writer, he was not writing for the childish, but for the childlike" (Raeper 305-306). MacDonald's growth in his writing complex characters and ideas can be seen through the development of his simple novel *The Princess and the Goblin*, onto its sequel, written eleven years later, entitled *The Princess and Curdie*, which has been described as "the most powerful of all MacDonald's books for children," as MacDonald forces his readers, both adults and children, to "wrestle with many difficult ideas" (Raeper 329). The book forces people to question what constitutes good and evil, and how one's choices and personal morals contribute to such ends. In it, goodness is now equated with death – goodness is seen as a complex and individual thing, and something that one must strive for constantly, as death comes to us all.

MacDonald was, perhaps subconsciously, influenced by his Scottish upbringing, and this awareness of Scotland's landscape and its folktales comes through in his writing. In Raeper's words: "The world of romance which MacDonald found in books as much as in hills and fir trees invades every corner of his novels. His books are interspersed with dreams, but also with ballads and poems [...]. Scottish folk tales and myths [...] held a twofold attraction for Mac-Donald. First, they enabled him to reach back into the world of his childhood to the traditions he had been cut off from by life in the city. In the Huntly of MacDonald's boyhood there were still kelpies lingering in rock pools, ghosts out haunting at night in Greenhaugh and Kinnoir, local witches who possessed the power to change them-selves into hares [...]" (Raeper 210). Although MacDonald claimed that he was influenced less by the wilder Scottish folktales and atmosphere than by more intellectual writ-ing, his argument does not come through in his writing, and his writing for childlike people can be considered more Scottish than other nineteenth-century children's authors who also wrote fantasy or fiction, such as J. M. Barrie (who invented the beloved character Peter Pan). MacDonald stated that "in each present personal being we have the whole past of our generation enclosed, to be redeveloped with endless difference in each individuality," and thus it is not surprising that "every now and then, into our consciousness float strange odours of feeling, strange tones as of by-gone affections, strange glimmers as of forgotten truths," as well as "strange mental sensations of indescribable sort and texture" (Raeper 210). This comment can be applied to MacDonald's writing, where one feels the Scottish influence behind it, rather than reads it directly. While his novels *The Princess and the Goblin, The Princess and Curdie* and *At the Back of The North Wind* are not set in any real city, it is easy to imagine them in a city like Edinburgh, as they reference not only urban settings but also castles, mountains and the sea. Edinburgh, for example, is famous for its historic castle, mountainous hill Arthur's Seat, and the nearby village of Cramond, where the Firth of Forth estuary flows out to the sea. MacDonald also weaves threads of Scottish folk beliefs, which often feature in folktales, into his novels, including in *At the Back of the North Wind* when Diamond's mother tells Diamond that his doing chores was a miraculous occurrence, similar to as if he had "been among the fairies" (MacDonald 383). This reference only makes sense if one has read Scottish folktales where fairies reward a hero with gifts or talents after he has lived among them. Raeper adds that "if MacDonald's novels appear divided – between Scottish and English, Gothic and Romance, real and fairy-tale – it is because he lived in a divided age and was trying to reconcile his own divided consciousness" (Raeper 213).

As much as one might like to argue that MacDonald fits into neat categories, his work, as well as the author himself, cannot be pigeonholed, either as just Scottish or just English, or that his works were just for children, and trying to fence him in only detracts from the brilliance that was his work. While MacDonald's fantasy novels are not "Scottish," in that they are not explicitly set in Scotland, there is still a Scottish air about them that does not appear in the best-known works of other Scottish novelists, such as J. M. Barrie. MacDonald's works do not shy away from the subject of children dealing with reality – in *The Princess and the Goblin* and its sequel, *The Princess and Curdie*, both the child protagonists are the only people in the kingdom to see evil within the kingdom, and to decide to fight against it. Likewise in *At The Back of The*

North Wind, while little Diamond loves escaping to the country at the back of the north wind, he also has no fear of helping an alcoholic neighbor with his miserable life, as well as driving a cab around London when his father becomes ill and is unable to support the family. The novel also confronts such grave topics as child neglect, misery, suicidal ideation, class divisions, substance abuse, as well as death.

While both Barrie and MacDonald have death as a theme in their works, MacDonald's child characters take on adult responsibilities with determination and hope, never shirking their duties, and never avoiding death through cowardice. This is in complete contrast to Barrie's *Peter Pan*, where the titular character states that he "ran away the day [he] was born [...] because he heard [his] father and mother talking of what [he] was to be when [he] became a man" (Barrie 99). Peter wants to always be a little boy, and never grow up.

Barrie's character Peter Pan's flight from the sinister villain Captain Hook may also be interpreted as the avoidance of adult life, for, apart from being a pirate, Hook's description mirrors that of an adult man in polite society. He is described as "never more sinister than when he is most polite, and the elegance of his diction, the distinction of his demeanour, show him one of a different class from his crew, a solitary among uncultured companions," and it is also said that "his courtliness impresses even his victims on the high seas" (Barrie 108). While Hook is menacing enough as a pirate, he is even more so if one reads him as the embodiment of adulthood attempting to kill that of childhood – Peter Pan. Some theatre and film productions of *Peter Pan* take this metaphor further, and have an actor who plays Mr. Darling also play Hook, wearing different costumes, signifying that there is a dark and menacing side to Mr. Darling, in a sense making him the father who wants to hurt and kill his children, just as Hook wishes Wendy hurt. Hook wants Wendy to watch her "children," i.e. her Lost Boys, to die, so that she will feel the intense pain of a mother (Barrie 140). Wendy acts calmly, asking Hook if "her children" are to die," and giving them a message on behalf of their real mothers, to die like "English gentlemen," presumably with courage and serenity (Barrie 140). This foreshadows the sentiments of the Darling children's real parents, who sit quietly grieving for their lost, presumed dead, children. Mr. and Mrs. Darling blame themselves, each in turn trying to reassure and comfort the other, but Mrs. Darling laments that "[she sees] them so often in [her] dreams that [she seems] still to see them when [she] is awake," and cries that "their silver voices call [her, her] little children whom [she'll] see no more" (Barrie 150). While Barrie's work is of the correct time period for this book, his imaginative world is so far-removed from Scottish influence or thought, and so it seemed best to use MacDonald more than Barrie for this study.

In reality, child death was more common in the nineteenth century in Scotland than it is today, due to the lack of affordable health care and effective medicine (antibiotics in particular). Yet research indicates that childhood had, by then, come to be seen by the middle and upper classes as a time of purity and innocence, when children should be unburdened by the troubles of everyday life. Due to this changing view, child death grew more shocking over the course of the nineteenth century, especially among the educated. The working class had no such luxury to give their children, as many poor Scottish children were forced to work just as hard as adults, or even harder, in mines and mills. Some children were proud to be able to work in order to support themselves or help their families financially, and even when they knew the dangers such employment could bring, it did not change their sentiments. MacDonald's fictional character Curdie is a representation of such a child, and the author's inclusion of such a child, a poor miner, as the protagonist of the novel *The Princess and Curdie*, demonstrates MacDonald's willingness to place a working-class child on the same level as the wealthy and innocent Princess Irene, thus defying consciousness of social classes. This is one reason why the novel has aged well over time, as its examinations of class discrimination, poverty, wealth, greed, tyranny, government, and death are timeless topics (and concerns for any individual in modern societies).

Victorian class differences in the UK (southern Scotland and England's urban areas) are described even more bluntly in MacDonald's *At The Back of the North Wind* and these class differences also demonstrate different children's beliefs. An example of this is where Diamond meets a little girl who works as a street sweeper, and although she is only a month or so older than Diamond, she calls him a child, only as the narrator describes it, "she had had to work for her bread, and that so soon makes people older" (Mac-Donald 339). When Diamond marvels at the young girl's courage and strength of character, she answers that "it is a life to be tired of – what with [her abusive guardian] old Sal, and so many holes in [her] shoes" (MacDonald 340). MacDonald then allows the little homeless girl a statement that also sums up his views on death as a new adventure, which Diamond embraces by the end of the novel, saying, "'When I think of it, I always want to see what's coming next, and so I always wait until next is over [...]'" (Mac-Donald 340). These juxtaposed views of childhood, of the innocent child and the working child, common to Victorian England and Scotland, are often juxtaposed with the representations of children in folktales, customs and fairy tales common to the two countries.

MacDonald was one of the nineteenth-century authors who was most influenced by the subject of child death, and this comes through in his works. While his books depict death as a generally positive aspect of human experience, as a transformation and something to be unafraid of, many scholars have since criticized him for romanticizing death, for ensuring that many of his protagonists have to die, or face near-death experiences, in order for their story's plot to move on or have a definitive conclusion. Kimberley Reynolds, for instance, describes in "Fatal Fantasies: the Death of Children in Victorian and Edwardian Fantasy Writing" how the "most complex and disturbing [attitude] to the death of children [is] found" in MacDonald's work, similarly to J. M. Barrie's Peter Pan, and that both MacDonald and Barrie's writing "in some way celebrates, demands, and presents as desirable the death of its child protagonist(s)" (Reynolds 171). *At The Back of the North Wind* "[calls] attention to the plight of the honest poor and [extols] their virtues," but the novel gives an explanation for child death that is problematic: that "Diamond clearly belongs to the group of children who 'like to die'" (Reynolds 174). This was a terrifying idea for parents, who, as Reynolds states, "had the difficult task of balancing the need to comfort dying children and their siblings with comfortable words about the next life with the need to keep their energies and aspirations firmly in the real world" (Reynolds 174).

While MacDonald and other authors tried to reconcile their own experiences of adult and child death with their devout Christian acceptance of death as a positive entrance into Heaven, other nineteenth-century writers, such as reporters evidently did not feel at ease discussing the controversial topic of death. Many articles in the nineteenth-century Scottish press, including the *Caledonian Mercury* and the local newspapers of Aberdeen, experienced difficulties in their attempts to be positive about child death, even when they wrote that the deceased child had "gone to Heaven." It is clear that children were seen as innocent beings, and their untimely deaths, regardless of circumstances and social status, were portrayed as tragic losses. This view influenced the way most modern Scottish and English people view death, and it paved the way for twentieth-century obituaries of children in newspapers.

3

DEATH IN SCOTTISH FOLKTALES

Folktales, myths and legends exist in every society, but every group's tales are both parallel and distinctive at the same time. They mirror each other and exist as opposites. Many Scottish tales make no reference to children at all, but of those I was able to find, child death is often viewed as transformative, a new experience, and one where death is not considered an ending in itself. In others, such as "Mally Whuppie," a child protagonist must face their own death, and sometimes kill others, in order to be rewarded – one questions the morals that children might learn, hearing or reading tales such as these. Scottish folktales also include tales of changelings, where adults, usually mothers, find that their human child has been replaced by a fairy changeling, and often have to kill the changeling in order to get their child back. In all of these tales, the reality and brutal nature of death, as an ending of someone's life, is never considered.

The folktales and customs that are centered on childhood death often concern infants, partly for religious reasons but also, no doubt, because the mortality rate was highest for the newly born. Scottish folktales that include young children as characters are often "full of anxiety and dread," as they focus on "the newborn or very young infant, someone who as yet has no firm place in the human community" (Avery and Reynolds 11). This made people feel nervous, as such infants were seen as "particularly vulnerable to supernatural dangers in life and [had] an ambiguous and potentially threatening status after death" (Avery and Reynolds 11). While many Christian people hoped and prayed for children to end up in heaven, fears over the certainty of that can be glimpsed in folktales and customs surrounding childhood death (Avery and Reynolds 11). Many anxieties over death, particularly childhood death, were due to the complexities, the rules and regulations, involved in the complex funeral procedures of the Christian faith in the nineteenth century

(Gordon 144-145). This was applicable to both England and Scotland, although Scottish Calvinists had a particularly strict doctrine, stating that everything in life was preordained by God, and only those select few that He had chosen (i.e. those few He deemed good enough) were able to go to Heaven (Applebaum 326). Most nineteenth-century English and Scottish people still believed that a proper burial was necessary to "ensure the repose of the dead," but this became problematic when children died, as Christian regulations refused to have unbaptized children, miscarried fetuses, and stillborn babies laid to rest in holy ground (Avery and Reynolds 11). Such children were often buried in paupers' graves, placed illegally in adult graves, or buried illegally on church grounds, or in nearby farmland, woods, or meadows, by grieving parents.

Even when people took measures to baptize their dead child themselves, and then bury them in consecrated ground, or place them secretly in adult graves, worries and fears surrounding the deaths and burials still influenced the songs, ballads and tales of the time, more so in England than in Scotland. While England's ballads and tales include positive depictions of dead children who return as moths or butterflies, there are also more ambiguous, or even troubling, representations of dead children returning as will-o-the-wisps, tiny lights which, although pretty, can guide travelers to their deaths, or sinister birds or mournful haunting ghosts (Avery and Reynolds 13). An example of this is the belief in South Somerset that "spunkies," or will-o-the-wisps, are the souls of unbaptized children, "doomed to wander until Judgement Day" (Palmer 244). Classic English literature includes representations of the anxieties felt by parents of unbaptized children; for example, in Thomas Hardy's *Tess of the d'Urbervilles*, the titular character Tess has her child, aptly called "Sorrow," after having been raped, and when the child dies, she is forced to baptize and bury it herself, as her child was born out of wedlock, and was thus shunned by Christian society. Hardy was clearly sympathetic to the plights of those who endured such circumstances, as he wrote it into his titular heroine's novel.

Scottish literature, however, appears to be comparatively silent on the topic. One possible explanation for the lack of Scottish folktales discussing child burials and deaths is that Scottish people often believed in fairies and spirits, and feared that if they spoke of the ghosts of the dead, or mourned their passing for too long, ill fortune might fall upon them. Most Scottish tales mention that one of the characters has died, but provide the minimal details only, leaving modern scholars to wonder why people were so close-mouthed. In James Hogg's "Adam Bell," it is mentioned that the titular character's father died when the titular character was just an infant, and that his mother died when he was twenty (Hogg 125). While it is obvious that these details serve only to move the plot along, by providing Bell with an inheritance, one wonders why the deaths are glossed over in such a way. While one might make the argument that Calvinist doctrine stopped some Scottish people from being able to grieve openly, as everything in life was pre-ordained by God, further research on Scottish folktales, ballads and poems contradicts such a clear-cut explanation (Applebaum 328).

The Scottish folktales and ballads, like the English, "indicate a profound guilt and unease," on the topic of death in general, often childhood death, and many touching on the latter are "specifically concerned with the punishment of the mothers responsible for the child's death – though never [...] of the fathers" (Avery and Reynolds 15). One Scottish folktale which uses this plot device is Elizabeth Grierson's version of "The Milk-white Doo," part of Gordon Jarvie's edited work *Scottish Folk and Fairy Tales*, (1992), which depicts an anxious father remarrying, in order to protect his children, and ironically, it is the children's new stepmother who murders the son (Grierson 9). Presumably, the first wife had died, as the father is anxious that the children have a new mother as soon as possible. It is common to folktales that one loving mother must die, in order for the cruel stepmother to take her place. Such tropes are evident in the now-famous fairytales such as Snow White, Cinderella (also known as Ashputtel), and others. The stepmother in "The Milk-white Doo" is described as a "most deceitful woman, who really [hates] children, although she pretended, before her marriage, to love them," and she treats her stepchildren so badly that their father wished he had not married her (Grierson 9).

As the tale follows the plot device of the murderous mother/stepmother, though, it follows that she must be evil, but is also denied a voice to explain her actions. One night, when the stepmother cooks a hare stew for her family, she begins to taste it, and due to her greed, eats all of it (Grierson 10). She feels so ashamed about this that she decides to remedy her mistake, but instead of apologizing to her husband (nothing is said of a possible apology to the children), or making another, simpler, meal, she re-sorts to murder, by hitting her stepson on the head with a hammer, to knock him out, and then boiling him alive in the stew pot (Grierson 10). The entire family sits and eats the stew, wondering all the while where the boy is, but the husband begins to doubt his wife's behavior when he finds his stepson's foot in his bowl (Grierson 10). This is a story that combines child death with the human capacity for evil, for the stepmother is a villain, as all folktales' and fairytales' stepmothers are portrayed as.

While this folktale is admittedly disturbing and brutal, it is one of the best examples in Scottish folktales of death as transformation. The stepson, Curly-locks, does not die a lasting death, but returns as a milk-white Doo, a dove, after his sister, guessing what had happened to him, gathers his bones and buries him in the garden (Grierson 10-11). The transformation is described in verse, as the bones "grew and grew, / to a milk-white Doo, / that took its wings, / and away it flew" (Grierson 11). It is a reminder of how important a proper burial was for many nineteenth-century Scottish people, as the tale implies that Curly-locks was only able to transform into a bird because his loving sister managed to gather *all* of his bones and bury them properly, together in one place (Grierson 10). This echoes the traditional Christian belief in the resurrection of the body. The tale implies that if the sister had accidentally left out one of her brother's bones when she buried them, that he would not have been able to come back as a Heavenly dove.

Both of the children are denied voices and opinions, due either to their purity, innocence, or their unimportance as children. Yet after Curlylocks' death and subsequent transformation into a bird, he is not only given a voice but uses it to wreak his revenge on his cruel stepmother, as well as provide gifts for his loving father and sister (Grierson 12-13). As a bird, Curly-locks flies to two women who are washing clothes, and tells them, "Pew, Pew, / My mimmie me slew, / My daddy me chew, / My sister gathered my banes, / And put them between two milk-white stanes. / And I grew and grew / To a milk-white Doo, / And I took to my wings and away I flew" (Grierson 11). As a reward for singing its tale, the bird receives a gift of clothing from the women, and later on, having sung the same song to a man counting silver and two millers, is given a bag of silver and a millstone in gratitude (Grierson 12-13).

One is not told why a bird should go to such lengths to obtain objects it cannot use, as a bird, but all becomes clear when the reader realizes it is a tale about revenge. This is shown by the bird going home to drop the millstone on his stepmother's head, thereby killing her (Grierson 14). He also rewards his father and sister, ostensibly for being the moral, loving people they are, by giving them clothing and silver, to ensure their financial security and happiness in the future (Grierson 14). The bird is never seen again after that, which makes it clear that the boy was transformed into a Heaven-sent being, intent on one sole purpose – getting his revenge on those who wronged him, and helping those who loved him. The cautionary tale certainly served as a warning to nineteenth-century stepmothers and mothers to be kind to those whom they are meant to protect and love. It also urged such step-mothers and mothers to fit into their accustomed roles and not cheat or lie to their families, or else they would be punished.

While the tale is also meant to amuse and entertain its listeners (as shown by its inclusion in the chapter "Fireside Nursery Stories" by the nineteenth-century author Robert Chambers in his work *Popular Rhymes of Scotland*), it has a warning tone and also serves as one of the best examples of death as transformation in Scottish nineteenth-century folktales and literature (Chambers 48-49). Grierson's version is written in English, while Chambers' is told in broad Scots, and it was likely that both versions circulated around Scotland, both among those who spoke Scots, where it would have been an oral tale, and those who spoke English, where it was probably written down. Perhaps similar versions of folktales travelled around different areas of Scotland, as well as different language groups, without the story being changed substantially. Chambers also comments that "it is curious to find out that this story, familiar in every Scottish nursery [during the nineteenth century], [was] also prevalent in Germany, where it [was] called *Machaudel Boom*, or the Holly Tree" (Chambers 50-51). These multiple versions show the major role of stories of childhood death in Europe at the time.

Many children in Scottish folktales are denied a voice and an opportunity to change their fate, others are given both, but must face the possibility of their own deaths, and many react with courage and resourcefulness. These few are able to triumph over adversity and secure positive futures for themselves; however, these triumphs often come at a fatal price to others. In the Scottish story, "Auld Cruivie," similar to its English counterpart, "Jack and the Beanstalk," Jack is a boy who angers a wealthy and greedy laird, or landowner – Jack is able to climb to safety but the greedy laird dies at the end of the tale. One can therefore read such child protagonists' lives as being more valuable than those they triumph over, usually monsters or other non-human beings. In order for the child to succeed, the villain must die, and unlike the child's transformative or moral, good death, the villain's death is always final. One Scottish tale where a young girl is featured as the heroine of the tale, and is able to take charge of her own actions and save herself is the story "Mally Whuppie," originally told in Aberdeenshire (120 Montgomerie). Unlike many other children in folktales who have no control over their own destinies, little Mally saves not only herself but her two older sisters as well, when threatened with imminent death (Montgomerie 121-122).

Mally Whuppie is first threatened with death at the start of the tale, when her poverty-stricken parents realize that they cannot afford to feed all their children. Their brutally cruel solution is to get rid of the three youngest girls by leaving them in a wood to fend for themselves and, in all likelihood, starve to death. The girls soon think that they are in luck when they stumble upon a house, but they soon find that the kind giantess who lives there has a husband who will kill them, given the chance. When the human girls are put to sleep in the bed where the giant's own children sleep, the giant puts straw necklaces on his guests and gold ones on his own daughters. Realizing that he means to harm his guests, the intelligent young Mally Whuppie secretly exchanges the necklaces, and so when the giant creeps in to beat his guests, he actually beats his own children. The pain of the giant children is merely a plot device put in to demonstrate the cunning and courage of Mally Whuppie in avoiding her own death, and saving the lives of her beloved sisters.

When the human girls escape and run to a nearby King's palace, Mally bravely goes back, facing her own possible demise thrice more, in order to steal (or "claim" for the king) the giant's sword, purse and ring. She does so to ensure the future happiness of her sisters and herself, for in gratitude for her bravery and thievery, the king marries off his sons to Mally Whuppie and her older sisters. The resourceful girl does express regret when the giant, trying to hurt her, accidentally beats his own wife instead. Mally

Whuppie runs away so that the giant himself might fol-low her, and in doing so, stop hurting his spouse. This demonstrates the girl's compassion for those that might have wronged her, an emotion rarely seen in folktales. Mally is a brave heroine, but she possesses the traits of the ideal feminine girl and the Victorian innocent child. Having faced the possibility of dying multiple times, Mally Whuppie triumphs by using her intellect, courage and quick thinking to save herself. She also triumphs over the thought of death, and while causing grief to villains, still embodies the idea of the self-sacrificing death – someone who happily faces death in order to help others.

The idea of someone embracing death in order to help another is turned on its head when it comes to Scottish folktales' depictions of changelings. These are usually sit-uations where adult fairy beings replace babies or tiny chil-dren with their own fairy infants or young children, steal-ing away the human child in the process to be raised with the fairies as guardians. Often the child's human parents quickly become aware of the changeling replacing their own child, and try to get rid of the changeling by threatening it with death or harming it so badly that it flees. The parents hope that the fairies will return their human child in return. Many of the measures parents go to get rid of changelings are brutal, and if one considers performing such acts on innocent human children, they would amount to horrific torture and infanticide. Changelings in folklore are traditionally fairies, non-human infants, who are often described as non-verbal, displaying many of the traits of autistic children, as they experience sensory overload, are unfortunately misunderstood by the adults around them, who do not understand them. As an autistic, disabled adult myself, these tales were especially hard to read when I was younger (and didn't yet have any diagnoses, but was aware of how uneasy I felt, and how similar the changelings' descriptions felt like me – now, as an adult with many diagnoses of various disabilities, it is heartbreaking). Autistic people deserve as much care and compassion as allistic (i.e. non-autistic) people.

Other changelings are described in folktales as "fretful and troublesome; often, they eat greedily but never seem satisfied;" and they often look physically different from other human infants, being "hairy, wrinkled, or very thin, or with a huge head" (Avery and Reynolds 24). Folklorists and other researchers today have been able to identify such descriptions in British folktales as being those of disability symptoms in children, including "progeria (premature aging, wrinkles, frail limbs) [...] and homocystinuria (weak, elongated limbs and hands)," among other classifications (Avery and Reynolds 24). While the tales generally describe the parents as being glad to rid themselves of the fairy being, it is difficult to know whether or not they truly believed the creature was not theirs, or if they were simply trying to dispose of a baby that they could not believe was their own, and needed such tales to persuade themselves that what they were doing was justified, not torture or murder. In the folktales, when the parents attempted to rid themselves of the changeling in various ways, the "fairywoman would then appear, rescue her own child, and give back the human one she had stolen," whereas "in real life, anybody following the procedures indicated would almost certainly cause the death of the disabled infant, but would feel no guilt, since the 'success' of the ritual would prove that the infant had not been human at all" (Avery and Reynolds 25). Such concepts are chilling to think about, as they echo the rhetoric that many modern people use to persuade themselves that discriminatory laws against disabled people are justifiable, even if it causes serious harm to people's lives. Once people see others as expendable, to be easily gotten rid of, they can justify their reprehensible actions to themselves and others. Real-life examples include the experiments that Hitler and his allies performed on disabled people in Nazi-governed Germany, in World War Two. As a disabled and autistic adult myself, it is chilling and horrifying to think about what happened to disabled and autistic children throughout history.

Examples of changeling lore in Scottish folktales include the stories "Torr-a-Bhuilg," "The Fostering Fairy's Lullaby" and "The Glengarry Fairy," all found in Reverend James MacDougall's collection *Folk Tales and Fairy Lore: In Gaelic and English*, first published in 1910. The tales both adhere to the standard depiction of changelings in folktales as well as provide valuable insight into the fairies' sentiments regarding the stolen child. Some tales, such as "The Changeling and the Fond Young Mother," are also moral tales, hinting to parents that if they are too proud and boastful, bad luck will come to them, perhaps in the form of fairies replacing their child with a changeling (Nic Leodhas 111). "Torr-a-Bhuilg" involves a housewife who cannot figure out what is wrong with her child, and it is only when a poor woman passes by the house and gives her advice, that she discovers that her child has been replaced with a fairy changeling (MacDougall 101). She reacts quite calmly to the news, in MacDougall's concise version, merely asking the poor woman what she ought to do (MacDougall 101). This version provides a much more humane approach to getting the changeling to leave, compared to other folktales, stories, and ballads of the time.

It is lucky for the changeling that the poor woman's advice does not involve harming and injuring it – merely startling it into revealing itself (MacDougall 101). The housewife places eggs in a circle on the floor, telling the changeling that she is making a "brewing caldron," to which the surprised fairy being responds, "I am more than three hundred years old, and I never yet saw a brewing caldron like that!" (MacDougall 101). Knowing then that her child had indeed been replaced with a fairy, the woman then pretended that the fairy settlement, Torr-a-Bhuilg, was on fire, and the anxious changeling ran out of the door, crying for its possessions, its bellows, anvil and hammers, never to be seen again (MacDougall 101). The method of getting rid of unwanted fairies is similar to that in the tale "The Good Housewife and her Night Labours," in Lord Archibald Campbell's *Waifs and Strays of Celtic Tradition*, first published in 1889, where a woman foolishly asks for help, soon receives a surprise visit from a crowd of fairies, but cannot get them to leave, until she cries that Burg Hill is on fire, and the fairies soon run to secure their possessions, crying:

"My wife and little ones, / My cheese and butter-keg, / My sons and daughters, / My big meal chests, / My comb and wool-cards [...], / My hammers and anvil, / Burg Hill is on fire; / And if Burg Hill is burnt, / My pleasant occupations / And merriments are gone" (Campbell 65).

In the tale "The Glengarry Fairy" the child's mother has no time for mercy, although she is merely in keeping with the standard for changeling treatment, as when she finds the being with "two teeth in his mouth, each more than an inch long, [and with a face] as old and withered as any face she had ever seen," she runs and throws it into a deep pool. It can be presumed that the mother is in mourning already, for she is described as a widow, and the loss of her child after having already lost her husband would cause her to be angry and sorrowful (MacDougall 117).

The tale "The Fostering Fairy" is an unusual poem, or lullaby, spoken from the fairy to her stolen human child (MacDougall 105-107). The fairy reminisces about the night she snatched the human baby from its home, saying how " [...] a-searching / Went wives from the steading / [...] Like rain tears shedding, / The lost child wailing, / The wild wood trailing [...]" (MacDougall 107). While the fairy admits to having caused the humans pain, she also demonstrates her happiness at having the child as her own, calling the infant, "'My joy! my treasure bright! / I stole thee one midnight: / Without candle, candlestick, / Light of heaven, light of earth, / Stole I thee from thy place of birth" (MacDougall 107). The fairy then reveals that she has had the child with her for a year, and to her it is "treasure to glad [her]" (MacDougall 107). It is evident that the fairy truly considers the human child to be hers, as she informs the child that within the year, [he] will be, "'On my shoulders 'bout the steading: / Thou art my darling, warlike, mail clad,'" and the fairy also reveals that the child is "[her] hope [...], / [Her] life and gladness" (MacDougall 107). Contrary to the typical notion of the evil fairy spiriting away the human child, this folktale, told in the form of a lullaby, shows that the fairy merely wanted the human child to raise as her own, and wanted to care for him properly as a mother. Perhaps tales of this sort gave hope and consolation to parents who feared that their child was gone forever, if the child vanished suddenly, or died unexpectedly. Such parents would likely have grieved the loss of their child(ren), but also found comfort and solace in the idea that their child was live somewhere, living with fairies in a magical land.

Scottish folktales which do feature child death often portray it as a transformation, as in "The Milk-white Doo," or "The Glengarry Fairy." Other folktales feature children who perform admirable deeds, or kill others out of desperation but not malice, as in "Mally Whuppie." Such folktales were significant not only because they often passed from person to person, through word of mouth, but they also travelled over a large geographical area, and the stories survived, even when the languages changed. The stories continued to be familiar to people, even when everything around them had become increasingly more urbanized, or events had changed the world, for example, during the Highland clearances, when approximately 70,000 Scottish Highlanders and Islanders were forcibly removed from their houses, possessions, and land, by wealthy landowners, over a one hundred year period of time. Many of these people died, while others survived, with many moving to the lands that are now known as Canada, the United States, Australia, New Zealand, or continental Europe. When people moved away from Scotland, they took their tales and stories, not to mention histories, with them. While some tales died out, these tales about child death remained, giving people insights into their own mortality.

One person who was influenced by them was George MacDonald, who used the idea of death as a good thing, a transformation, or a new adventure, in his novels, particularly the work *At the Back of The North Wind*, which I discuss later on. It is difficult though, to examine MacDonald's writings about child death without first looking at MacDonald's own life, which I examine in the next chapter, along with contrasting his experience with a child diarist, Marjory Fleming, one of the few Scottish child authors from the nineteenth century whose work has survived.

4

SCOTTISH PEOPLE'S ACCOUNTS OF CHILD DEATH

Insights into child death in Scottish culture can be explored through biographical records. When one thinks of George MacDonald (1824-1905), one gains a much better perspective on the works when one considers MacDonald's own experiences. Apart from struggling with his faith, George MacDonald also had a difficult time dealing with death, as he stood by helplessly and watched many of his loved ones die, at various points throughout his life. He had to endure this as a child, and then again as an adult, when two of his own children died. Another young Scot, Marjory Fleming, died aged eight, but before she did, wrote her now-famous diaries, discussing her thoughts on everything but death. Even four days before she died, she remained hopeful, writing poems to please her loved ones, refusing to admit she might die.

MacDonald's experiences as a child show that children are just as affected by death as adults are, even if they are not able to be as vocal and expressive about it. David S. Robb writes that MacDonald could never have been "long free from the knowledge of human mortality and transience: not only was his own death an ever-present possibility, but he had to bear the loss of many of those dearest to him," including his mother, who died early in his life, his father and brother, who passed away in the 1850s (Robb 16). MacDonald was influenced by death from an early age, as his "earliest definable memory [was] of a great funeral of one of the Dukes of Gordon, when [he] was between two and three years of age," and while, as Raeper writes, MacDonald "was too young to associate the splendid melancholy of the funeral cortège with the reality of death, this memory may have served as a kind of omen, for death's shadow flitted in and out of MacDonald's long life" (Raeper 25). Many of MacDonald's family died of tuberculosis, and he experienced such tragedy often enough that MacDonald "came to refer to the disease as 'the family attendant'" (Raeper 25). MacDonald used his writing to deal with his emotions and memories, as in *Ranald Bannerman's Boyhood*, the titular character "remembers his mother bending over a baby – then, when he woke up, both the baby, his mother and the cradle were gone, [and] in this way, the young boy knew that the baby was dead" (Raeper 28). William Raeper, MacDonald's biographer, believes this is MacDonald's only memory of his brother John, who "died in infancy," put down in words (Raeper 28). George MacDonald also experienced one of the greatest losses of his life when his mother died when he was only eight years old. She died of tuberculosis, leaving behind "only a miniature, a lock of hair, and a few fragments of memory" (Raeper 32). Biographer Raeper states that while "time washed over [MacDonald's] loss [there] is a silence about [his mother Helen] which is very deep and hard to penetrate" (Raeper 32). It appears likely that the MacDonald children did not receive much affection or love from their father after the death of their mother, and biographer Raeper believes that MacDonald consoled himself by reading (Raeper 32). Raeper also likens Mac-

Donald's early fascination with death to the narrator of *The Portent*, also by MacDonald, who stated:

"I used to look forward with expectation to the hour when, laying myself straight upon my back, as if my bed were my coffin, I could call up from underground all who had passed away, and see how they fared, yea what progress they had made towards final dissolution of form" (Raeper 33).

Raeper hypothesizes that "this rather morbid, graphic fascination with death is probably understandable in a lonely, bookish boy who has tasted death at an early age" (Raeper 33). When MacDonald grew up and fell in love with Louisa Powell, their happiness was soon tainted by the sudden deaths of Louisa's cousin and aunt, which frightened and shocked Louisa, bringing home to her the reality of death, despite MacDonald's efforts to comfort her throughout their lives together (Raeper 71). Relatively soon after, in 1850, Louisa's mother died of "the family attendant," tuberculosis, leaving Louisa "distraught [but assured and comforted by MacDonald's words] on the power and certainty of the love of God" (Raeper 75). The Powells' views on death adhered to the standard opinion of the time, that death "was the entrance to an eternity of

days, that is, that souls went on existing in endless time,"
and this did not comfort them a great deal (Raeper 76).
MacDonald had much more optimistic views on death,
however, views which influenced his writing. He believed
that "death was a birth into something *better* and so [it]
was a hopeful sign, a sign of God's unalterable promise
and unfailing love – a *good* sign," and he took great pains
to communicate this to the Powell family, hoping to help
them in their distress (Raeper 76).

George MacDonald is a fascinating case study as his life
provides information on both children and adults reacting
to child death. Another child who can provide valuable
insight on child death in Scotland is Marjory Fleming
(1803-1811), the youngest person to date who is listed in
the Dictionary of National Biography. Marjory is a fine
example of how "naturally light-hearted children [can be],
and how difficult it [often] is to fix their minds on serious
matters" (Avery 106). George MacDonald, as a child, is
one notable exception to this view – he focused on death
a lot as a child. Marjory Fleming, by contrast, is one of
the only child diarists to think about death without reli-
gion's influence. Many other children at the time had been
influenced "by their upbringing to look beyond death,

either with happy anticipation," or else fear (Avery 107). As Gillian Avery writes, in her essay, "Intimations of Mortality: the Puritan and Evangelical Message to Children," Marjory is a child who does not believe in death as she knows she ought to, as she "knows what she ought to think, but the reckless Marjory, living only for the present, keeps breaking through" in her writing (Avery 107).

She writes about her hatred of mathematics, stating in her journal, "'I am now going to tell you about the horible and wretched plaege that my multiplication gives me you cant concieve it – the most Devilish thing is 8 times 8 & 7 times 7 it is what nature itselfe cant endure'" (Macbean 54). Death as reality is something which the then six-year-old Marjory could not fully imagine, as in her second journal, she wrote, "'A sarvant tried to piosen mistress & 2, 3 children, what a dreadful concience she must have'" (Macbean 59). When she was seven, in her third journal, Marjory wrote how much she enjoyed reading such Gothic novels as *The Mysteries of Udolpho*, and *The Monk*. She also wrote, "Death the righteous love to see / but from it doth the wicked flee / I am sure they fly as fast as their legs can carry them" (Macbean 75).

When Marjory caught measles the November before her death, it appears this led to her getting meningitis, and dying from it that December. Four days before she died, she wrote a poem in her third, and last, journal, describing her thoughts. The poem was called "Address to dear Isabella on the Authors recovery," and Marjory writes, "'Oh! Isa pain did visit me/ I was at the last extremity/ How often I did think of you/ I wished your graceful form to view/ To clasp you in my weak embrace/ Indeed I thought I'd run my race [...]'" (Macbean 114). Marjory's last wish, before she died, was that she might regain enough strength to go out and buy a present for her cousin, Isa, for New Year's, using the sixpence she had been given by the doctor (Macbean 112). This demonstrates little Marjory's childish hopefulness, even when dying, and her refusal to admit that she might not get better. While her story is tragic, the little eight-year-old was able to remain hopeful, even when dying, and her suffering does not appear as great as that of the adult MacDonald, who felt he only understood death when, as a parent, he had to bury two of his own children in the same year.

Although George MacDonald had had to experience a great deal of death in his life, especially as a child, it was not until two of his own eleven children died that he felt it to be overwhelming and final. He had tried to think of death as a positive experience; now it really shocked him (Raeper 344-345). In 1877, after being informed by the doctor that their daughter Mary needed a winter abroad, the MacDonalds took her to the Riviera, as it was either face the "difficult move, or their daughter's death" (Raeper 339). Unfortunately, Mary's health worsened, so much so that MacDonald had to prepare his wife for the worst, telling her that, "'We cannot keep Mary if her Father wants her, but we can trust him and go on'" (Raeper 340). While MacDonald knew that his daughter was beyond hope, and was dying, as he had already seen many of his other family members die, it still affected him deeply.

Mary died at twenty-four, after growing steadily weaker, but she was still MacDonald's child, and "the white silk that was to have been her wedding dress became [the] pall" for her coffin (Raeper 342). His wife Louisa took her daughter's death harder than her husband, for MacDonald himself had managed to regain his health after many serious illnesses, but now it was her daughter who was gone, and this left Louisa feeling numb, and she was "tormented at being parted from her child" (MacDonald 342).

MacDonald tried to console Louisa, including writing a poem which includes the lines:

"To tell thee that our blessed child

Is watching thee from somewhere nigh,

Mourns with thee when thy agony grows wild,

Sits sometimes by thy bed while slow the hours go by

[...]" (Raeper 342).

The couple then had to endure another blow – that of the death of their son, Maurice, aged fourteen or fifteen (1864-1879). In February 1879, he quickly "succumbed to pneumonia, and died in the short space of eighteen days" (Raeper 344). The boy had been ill all winter but had seemed to be on the mend; then he experienced a sudden hemorrhage, and although his mother anxiously devoted all her time to being his nurse over the next ten days, Maurice eventually died (Raeper 344). The boy "scarcely ever complained, but gave a weak smile," and eventually murmured, "'I have to remember that God is with me,'" multiple times, before "giving a little short sigh and ceasing to breathe" (Raeper 344). While Mary's death had been expected for a long time, in contrast, Maurice's was sudden and traumatic. George MacDonald later wrote to his stepmother in Aberdeen that "neither Louisa nor [he] knew much about death until these two were taken from us within the year – and now we know its terror and its comfort" (Raeper 344).

While MacDonald always tried to remain optimistic about life, Maurice's death sent him spiraling into despair. "Death, like high faith levelling, lifteth all. / When I awake, my daughter and my son, / Grown sister and brother, in my arms shall fall [...]" (Raeper 345). MacDonald had always felt that Maurice would be the son to be "destined for great things," and he is described by MacDonald's biographer, Raeper, as "the family's own Diamond," the saintly and pure child of MacDonald's earlier novel *At the Back of The North Wind* (Raeper 345). With the death of Maurice, all MacDonald's hopes and dreams for his sons also died, as Maurice had been the favorite son. One of Maurice's older brothers, Ronald, grew to resent his father; as shown in one surviving letter, Ronald describes his father telling his sons that none of them would ever amount to as much as their sisters, as well as taking his grief about Maurice's death out on them (Raeper 345). It is clear that people's reactions to the death of a child, especially those of the people who loved the deceased, are varied and complex, and that often feelings are hurt, leading to resentments and frustrations which might remain among families and friends forever, leading to arguments and rifts which might never be resolved.

Death continued to inspire and motivate MacDonald, as he used death as a plot device in many of his children's novels, which I will discuss later on. He also took death as a theme for his adult fantasy novel *Lilith*, stating that the hero cannot die unless he dies a good, i.e., moral and accepting, death. While I do not have the space to discuss *Lilith* at length, its theme can of the "good" death can also be used to interpret MacDonald's other works.

5

CHILD DEATH IN GEORGE MACDONALD'S LITERARY WORKS

Many Scottish authors have discussed the idea of death in their works, but perhaps none have given it so much attention as George MacDonald. Death is a central focus of many of his books, including the children's novels *The Princess and The Goblin*, published in 1872; its sequel *The Princess and Curdie*, published in 1883; *At the Back of The North Wind*, published in 1871; and his adult fantasy novel *Lilith*, published in 1895. In *The Princess and the Goblin*, it is clear that his ideas about death have been influenced, perhaps subconsciously, by Scottish folktales, where humans triumph over supernatural beings and forces, especially if the creatures are uglier or more hideous than they are – humans win simply by being what they are, human, not for who they are inside.

MacDonald's views change and grow when it comes to *The Princess and Curdie*, for there, monstrous creatures can be redeemed through good and moral actions, and evil humans can be punished because of their wrongdoing. MacDonald creates a more complex view of human and supernatural nature and death by having plots in which characters are punished for what they have done, and he does not condemn them simply for being who they are. In *At the Back of The North Wind*, the boy waif Diamond dies, but as he is assumed to have gone to the country at the back of the North Wind, this is seen as a good and necessary change, despite the grief his passing generates among those he leaves behind. MacDonald's books often depict death as a positive aspect of human experience and a transformation, leading to a new adventure.

In *The Princess and the Goblin*, the two protagonists, Princess Irene and Curdie, the miner boy, embody the two standard Victorian views of childhood, and are comforted by Irene's mysterious great-great-grandmother, who is essentially a type of goddess, immortal, wise, pure, and strong. The idea of her gives strength and courage to Curdie and Irene, and because they alone can see her, an immortal being, it makes them unafraid of death. The little princess Irene is the Victorian embodiment of a wealthy child, an innocent soul who is allowed to remain innocent, unburdened with the cares of adulthood. Curdie, the miner's son, is the Victorian embodiment of a working child; he labours in the mines to help support his family. Irene is first described as a sort of china doll, a "sweet little creature [...], her face fair and pretty, with eyes like two bits of night sky, each with a star dissolved in the blue" (MacDonald 1). She is kept innocent as she is denied the opportunity to do anything, even see the night sky, as the king's staff are too afraid of the goblins and other horrors that lurk in the night to let Irene do anything that might harm her.

It is only when she explores an unknown part of the castle, relies upon her own resources, and stumbles upon her great-great-grandmother, that she begins to grow as a character, then being described as "as brave as could be expected of a princess her age" (MacDonald 3). Irene's great great-grandmother describes herself as being "too old for [Irene] to guess" (MacDonald 6), tells her that no one else in the castle knows she is there, and when Curdie tries to meet her for the first time, he does not believe in her, and so is unable to see her. This can be explained due to his status as a child miner —as a twelve-year-old, he has taken on the responsibilities of an adult. Therefore, he has lost some of his innocence and purity of heart that Irene, a princess, has been allowed to retain.

The unbalanced levels of maturity change in *The Princess and Curdie*, however, when the princess is forced to care for her ill father amidst a castle full of traitorous servants, and thus grows into maturity more quickly than she otherwise would (MacDonald 132). MacDonald's faith comes through in the characters of Irene and Curdie – faith that everything will turn out right, and that good people will be rewarded, bad ones punished, and the repentant sinners given a second chance. The foundation of the children's faith is Irene's great-great-grandmother, who requires absolute trust, goodness, and obedience from those she protects. A similar trust of death comes through in many of MacDonald's other characters and works.

Irene's great-great-grandmother offers both protection and "good" deaths to those who believe in her, but such actions also require great strength on the part of the individuals who need her protection or her forgiveness. In *The Princess and Curdie*, she appears to Curdie looking much younger, dressed in green, and "the mother of all the light that dwells in the stones of the earth" (MacDonald 102). She is also able to pluck a large emerald embedded in rock, with her bare fingers, a feat Curdie describes as one which twenty men would fail to accomplish (MacDonald 102). Her transformative gifts are again shown when she asks Curdie to put his hands into a fire and trust her. Curdie "held the pain as if it were a thing that would kill him if he let it go – as indeed it would have done" (MacDonald 107).

His trust and courage are rewarded when this gives him the ability to clasp the hand of a man and see his inner being, whether it appears truly human, or if corrupt, to see the animal he is turning into. MacDonald writes that it is unbearable for a man to realize he is turning into a beast, for "he is ceasing to be a man [and] it is the dying man in him that makes it uncomfortable" (MacDonald 109). This statement demonstrates MacDonald's belief that unless a person is good and moral at heart, he or she cannot be happy, and there is even a hint that the man himself, if he is corrupt enough to be animalistic at heart, ought to die, in order to rid the world of his immorality. While MacDonald portrays other deaths as moral and therefore positive, he views the change from man to beast, in the corrupt humans, as a form of death, one that is tragic and regrettable (MacDonald 109). This is completely at odds with his portrayals of "good" deaths, such as that of the monster Lina.

In *The Princess and The Goblin* George MacDonald portrays the goblins as evil. One can see how Scottish folk-tales' depictions of monsters and giants influenced him, as their supernatural creatures are often shown to be evil, not by their actions, but merely by their being supernatural. Just as the giant in "Mally Whuppie" is a villain simply because he is a giant, so too are the goblins of *The Princess and the Goblin* evil because they are goblins.

MacDonald's views of good and evil change and grow, however, in *The Princess and the Goblin*'s sequel, *The Princess and Curdie*, as he allows individuals to be good or evil depending on the choices they make, and their result-ing actions, rather than simply being categorized by what species they happen to be. In *The Princess and Curdie,* he depicts one of the most monstrous characters ever created as capable of redemption and forgiveness, and most importantly in MacDonald's viewpoint, as deserving of a "good" death. Lina is described as a "horrible mass of incongruities [...], [with a] head [that is] something like that of a polar bear and a snake [...], [has dark green eyes], with a yellow light in them," and her "under teeth [come] up like a fringe of icicles, only very white, outside of her bottom lip" (MacDonald 110). Having described Lina's monstrous exterior appearance, MacDonald then shocks his readers by showing them her inner self, through Curdie holding her paw to see what manner of creature she is inside (MacDonald 110). Curdie holds Lina's paw, and immediately perceives "the soft, neat little hand of a child!" (MacDonald 110). Despite Lina's outward appearance, then, her inner self is filled with goodness, strength, and loyalty, as shown by her unwavering faith towards Irene's great-great-grandmother and Curdie.

Lina, having done her duty by Curdie, is allowed to die a "good" death, thereby showing that death can be given as a reward. After the battle is finally over, Curdie visits Irene's great-great-grandmother, and glimpses Lina "slowly wagging her tail," and almost unable to hold herself back from springing into the fireplace (MacDonald 167). Irene's great-great-grandmother is "casting roses, more and more roses, upon the fire [and she] then commands, "'Now Lina!'" and immediately Lina jumps, "burrowing [,] into the fire" (MacDonald 167). The result is "a black smoke and a dust," and Lina is never seen again (MacDonald 167). Lina, the ugliest and most frightening creature of the novel, is granted the last proper scene, demonstrating how important her reward, of dying a "good" death, or dying in order to undergo a transformation, is. MacDonald also reminds his reader how fleeting an experience life is, as at the end of *The Princess and Curdie*, he has the city Gwyntystorm literally collapse. Curdie and Irene have died, and the city's inhabitants have grown too greedy and have mined through the entire foundation, killing all who live there (MacDonald 167). MacDonald suggests that while a "good" death is something to be desired and cherished, a bad one accomplishes nothing, and those who die such a death do not deserve to be mourned properly.

MacDonald also portrays death as a positive experience in his earlier novel *At the Back of The North Wind*, where his main character, the frail Diamond, experiences grand adventures with the North Wind, but ultimately dies. It is a "good" death, as the narrator states that Diamond has merely gone "to the back of the north wind" (MacDonald 480). At the start of the novel, the reader is warned of Diamond's family's poverty: his parents live in a "low room over a coach-house," but as there is so little room for even a small boy there, Diamond is forced to sleep in the stable's loft, above the head of the old horse, whom the boy is named for (MacDonald 321). His bed is surrounded by thin boards, no more than "an inch thick, and on the other side of them was the north wind," which is able to get in through a hole in one of the boards (MacDonald 322). These descriptions foreshadow the fact that Diamond's lodgings are inadequate, posing a danger to his health and wellbeing, that his health will fail him, and that he does not have long to live.

The North Wind, similar to Irene's great-great-grandmother in *The Princess and Curdie,* is a source of mystery and shape-shifting power, although North Wind does not inspire the same level of trust. She first appears as a beautiful grown-up woman, and then as a young girl. One of her descriptions of herself is that of "the old woman who sweeps the cobwebs from the sky" (MacDonald 334). She also frightens people in order to teach them lessons, for when Diamond asks, she tells him, "'Good people see good things; bad people, bad things'" (MacDonald 334). When Diamond asks why she helped him but not a poor little urchin girl shivering in the street, the North Wind tells him that "everybody is not ready for the same thing," again suggesting that Diamond is slowly leaving the world he knew and is becoming immersed in another (MacDonald 336). This kind of language is also foreboding, suggesting the potential grooming of children by adults for their own purposes (a practice which unfortunately, continues to this day, and is echoed in the twentieth century C. S. Lewis novel *The Lion, The Witch and the Wardrobe* when the White Witch preys upon Edmund for her own purposes).

While it seems like a marvelous journey, the novel hints ominously at Diamond's future death. Even the title, *At The Back of the North Wind*, hints at it, and the meaning behind this gradually becomes clear, for example, when the North Wind tells Diamond that she must cause a ship to sink, and yet what seems like cruelty is not really so, that those she drowns are just carried away to the back of the North Wind (MacDonald 343). The North Wind's movements are at times beautiful, but at other times dangerous, for they are compared to the crashing of the sea's waves on rocks, only wilder. The North Wind is also shown to be a transformative goddess-like or fairy-like figure, though she inspires just as much fear in the hearts of adult men and women as she does goodness and hope in the heart of Diamond (MacDonald 474). North Wind admits to Diamond that while he sees her as a kind and motherly figure, she has other names which inspire terror in the hearts of men, such as "Bad Fortunes [or] Evil Chance," or even Ruin, and that "they have another name for [her] which they think the most dreadful of all" (MacDonald 474). It is implied that this name would be Death, or even as she is female and beautiful, perhaps the Angel of Death.

After Diamond's first few adventures with the North Wind, his frailty begins to show more and more, as his mother remarks that she does not think he looks well (MacDonald 355). The country at the back of the North Wind is not just represented as a heaven on earth, but is more complex, for when Diamond visits, he passes through a "cold [that] stung him like fire," and once there, was not quite happy, but was "still and quiet and patient and contented," feeling that it was "better than mere happiness," and that nothing could ever go wrong there (MacDonald 364-365). Diamond is often described as a sort of Christ-like figure (Raeper 307), and is called "God's baby," due to his size, frailty and youth, but most of all because of his angelic nature, wisdom, and purity (MacDonald 466). As such, it only makes sense if Diamond, like Christ, is fated to die at the end of the novel. When North Wind discusses her various names with Diamond, she asks him if he remembers having to go through her to get to the country at her back, and when he says yes, Diamond adds that she was very cold, and that his heart "grew like a lump of ice, and then [he] forgot for a while" (MacDonald 474). North Wind then hints that her other name might be Death, as she informs Diamond that while he was ice-cold and still, he was "very near knowing what they call [her] then" (MacDonald 474).

Diamond dies four days later. His corpse is described as "a lovely figure, as white and almost as clear as alabaster, lying on the bed" (MacDonald 480). The narrator sums up the novel's message in his and the others' reactions to Diamond's death: "They thought he was dead. I knew that he had gone to the back of the north wind" (MacDonald 480). The description of Diamond's corpse is similar to that of Marjory Fleming, whose mother wrote, "Never did I behold so beautiful an object. It resembled the finest waxwork. There was in the countenance an expression of sweetness and serenity which seemed to indicate that the pure spirit had anticipated the joys of heaven ere it quitted the mortal frame" (Macbean 116). Similar to most Scottish graves in Edinburgh for the time period, Marjory's grave, which rests in Abbotshall Churchyard, is very simple, bearing no verse or lines, just, "Pet Marjorie. / Marjorie Fleming. / Born 1803. Died 1811" (Macbean 116). Both Marjory's mother and the narrator of *At the Back of the North Wind* view death as an ascension to Heaven, which comforts them.

While many people, both in the nineteenth century and today, would like to believe that death is a transformation or a new adventure, it is clear that people have always struggled with this idea, for as much as they would like to believe it, they often cannot. In nineteenth-century Scottish newspapers, particularly the *Glasgow Herald* and the *Caledonian Mercury*, many articles featured child death occurrences, and while some reports stuck to the dominant Christian beliefs by saying that the dead child's soul would end up in heaven the news reports are often full of woe and regret. They portray child death as a tragedy, something that could have been prevented and ought to have been.

6

Child Death in Scottish Newspapers

Nineteenth-century Scottish newspapers appeared conflicted in their reports on child death. Their articles generally tried to accept such instances as God's will, but they also struggled with accepting such events, seeing them as losses of innocent beings, regardless of the dead child's social status. Scottish papers included many reports of child deaths, but most of those records and reports centered on the urban areas in southern Scotland, as the Highlands and Islands were less populated and more difficult to get to. As a result, the urban parts of southern Scotland had more newspaper circulation. The articles and obituaries bordered on sensationalist, and often journalists and officials used the deceased child to blame neglectful, often impoverished, parents, without considering the parents' circumstances and domestic conditions. Surprisingly though, considering the relative amount of silence surrounding the emotions aroused by child deaths in the nineteenth century, as shown by the comparative lack of documents in archives and libraries, some poems were published in the literary sections of newspapers about grieving for dead children. These poems were open about grief.

People grieve in various ways, and emotion often comes first, before rational thinking. Parents who lose their children want answers as to why their child had to die. "Alongside mourning, a basic human response to bereavement is to demand some explanation, to seek out someone or something to blame, especially in tragic and 'unnatural' circumstances such as a young child's death" (Avery and Reynolds 19). Any thought that mere accident is responsible is emotionally unsatisfying. "In centuries where infant mortality was common, a single death was not usually dramatic enough in itself to be a subject for storytelling and moralizing; if, however, there was anything abnormal or monstrous about the actual birth, this was readily seen as a supernatural event and interpreted as God's judgment on a sin of the parents; usually, of the mother" (Avery and Reynolds 19). This can be seen in various Scottish folktales, as discussed earlier, where horrified mothers try to kill changelings, in order to get their own child back. In "The Glengarry Fairy," for example, when the distraught mother throws the changeling into a deep pool, she hopes to get her own child in return; but in real life, she would doubtless commit infanticide. Such an event occurred in the demesne of Heywood, Ireland, in 1840.

It was reported in the *Caledonian Mercury* newspaper, under the headline "An Extraordinary Case of Gross Superstition," and told of a young boy who was badly beaten, and eventually died, having been labeled a changeling by his family. The boy, named John Mahony, had been confined to his bed for two years due to a spinal injury. He was accused of being a fairy, essentially a changeling, due to his intellectual nature and disconcerting habit of making "shrewd remarks about everything he heard and saw passing around him" ("Gross Superstition"). The article's headline shows where the press's sympathies lay, contrary to the Scottish and Irish folktales about changelings. It presents a very grim view: "the poor dying child was threatened with a red-hot shovel and a ducking under a pump, if he did not disclose where the real John Mahony was". It is clear that the boy was at his wits' end as to what to say, but eventually the weak and terrified child, after "having been held near the hot shovel, and also having been taken a part of the way to the pump, told them he was a fairy, and that he would send back the real John Mahony the next evening, if they gave him that night's lodgings." The article stated that this incident "occurred on Tuesday night last, and the child was dead the next morning." One on-looker, Mathew Tynan, was "so disgusted with the questions that [the others] were putting to the child" that he went away, but it does not look as if he tried to help the child further. This shows that while many Scottish and Irish folktales made intriguing headlines to read, people's belief in changelings could allow or even encourage adults to commit child murder.

In Scottish newspapers, many articles which discussed child death did so in a sensationalist way, providing all the details of gruesome cases. News reports today do the same thing. One example, from the *Caledonian Mercury*, was the case of Ann Semple, who was accused of murdering her infant daughter, on June 8, 1837, in Paisley, Scotland. The eight- or nine-month-old's body was discovered floating in the canal on June 14, dressed in a "frock and petticoat, with a string of glass beads around [its] neck" ("Glasgow Circuit Court"). The article makes it clear that the accused mother was desperate, as she had no money, and was often reprimanded by others for the lack of attention to personal care she gave to her child. The unnamed infant was described as "always hungry and craving for food". The father had been arrested for poaching (hunting animals illegally). The mother had lied about the child's death and told various witnesses it was buried in a churchyard. While Ann Semple was evidently disturbed, telling people of her happiness after her child's death, it is clear that the death affected her, as she was seen "on the street entering several shops in a very confused and agitated manner". The mother argued that she had only put the dead child into the canal after it had already died, as she had no money to pay for a proper burial. Lord Moncrieff then passed his sentence on her, that she was to be executed, and also reprimanded her, saying, "'You now stand convicted of the appalling crime of the murder of your own child – the child of your womb, which you brought into existence.'" He added that it was "[her] duty, as it [was] the earnest desire of most if not all mothers, to protect and cherish" their children, and she had killed hers ("Glasgow Circuit Court"). The judge admitted that he did not know what the woman's previous life was like – a telling statement, as it is made clear through the descriptions of her poverty, her husband's being arrested for poaching, and her inability to give her child proper food and care, that she perhaps felt she had no other choice – that the child's life would have been as miserable as hers.

In nineteenth-century society, desperate mothers who could not cope with their circumstances (including extreme poverty and numerous children, often born because of the lack of birth control, or stemming from sexual assaults, such as rapes) were shown little sympathy. Another court case, published in the *Caledonian Mercury*, was that of Marrion Murray, who in 1848 was charged with "child murder or concealment of pregnancy," as if the two accusations were to be weighed equally, and had, on the 22nd of June, "been delivered of a living male child on the turnpike road between Peebles and Traquair" ("Jedburgh Circuit Court"). The infant's body was eventually found, on July 9, still in the spot where the mother had given birth. The court examined the evidence and decided that "the manner of child's death or murder had not distinctly transpired," and so the accused mother was sentenced to nine months in the Peebles' jail for concealing her pregnancy, but nothing more. In these articles about murderous mothers the grim facts of the children's deaths are discussed in greater detail than the emotions and reactions of the accused mothers themselves. One wonders what the mothers were thinking when they realized their children were dead, but the articles rarely provide such information, only remarking on whether or not the accused mothers appear to feel indifferent or even confused yet happy, as in the case of Ann Semple, whose juxtaposed emotions, as described in the article, were interpreted as evidence of her culpability.

Those who lose children often react differently to what might be expected, as grief manifests itself in different ways for different individuals. An example of this is how, in the *Aberdeen Journal*, published on February 9, 1820, the paper reported the death of King George III. The article recalled a moment when one of his daughters was near death, and he was in the midst of reading a sermon to his family ("Death of His Most Excellent Majesty"). One of the king's attendants entered the room, bearing "tidings of the child's death," and the "King exchanged a look with him, signifying he understood his commission," but either out of duty, or being at a loss as to what he ought to do, still "proceeded with his reading until it was finished." While it is true that the article might have exaggerated the King's devotion to Christianity, in order to give readers a loyal portrayal of their monarch, it still gives us a brief glimpse of a confused and grief-stricken parent. But still, this is an example of how adults, especially parents, do not always react to the loss of their child in the way one might expect, i.e., accepting the loss instantly or crying openly. George III, when he heard his daughter had passed away, kept on reading the sermon to his family, perhaps allowing himself time before having to face the reality and gravity of the situation. Little diarist Marjory Fleming wrote, at the age of about eight, in her third journal, an ode to King George III, and thoughtfully remarked that "Poor man his health is very bad / and he is often very mad / he was a very comely lad / since death took his girl from his sight / he to her grave doth walk at night [...]" (Macbean 76). These simple, amusing lines, written by a little child, allow us to see that while perhaps the king was not the type to grieve instantly and emotionally, without first weighing the consequences of his actions, he did spend time thinking of, and visiting, his beloved girl who had passed away, or so the story went. Regardless of if it is true or not, the young child's thoughts allow us a glimpse into childish ideas about death and loyalty. It is an example of how loving parents everywhere take their child's death to heart, and how sorrow can feel the same regardless of where the person is, socially and geographically, in the world.

Some adults saw the reality of death all around them, and became inspired to write poetry, using it as an outlet for their emotions. Newspapers in the nineteenth century in Scotland occasionally printed poems about the topic as well as their somber articles. Such poems saw child death as a sorrowful tragedy but also a source of hope, stating that the child's soul would ascend to Heaven. One such poem, entitled "The Dying Boy," written by one K. J. from Edinburgh, and printed in the *Aberdeen Journal*, February 9, 1842, allows its readers to know a dying boy's sentimental thoughts in the minutes before he dies, and provides an optimistic view of death and beyond. The boy reminds his mother of "A quiet green spot of ground, / Where the moss and the wild rose grow thickly around, / And a tall broad oak in its grandeur throws / It's cool shade alike o'er the moss and the rose, / Far away from the hot sun's scorching glare," and asks her that "When [he] is dead, let [him] slumber there" (K. J. "Dying Boy"). As he is dying, he tells his mother that he hears a "distant hymn," sung by an angel, who "calls [him] away to a better home." This view is similar to that of George MacDonald – that death is a positive experience, that Heaven, or whatever comes next, is a better place than Earth, and that it is a new adventure.

A second poem, which is simultaneously bleak and hopeful, called "The Dying Child," by one A. Gordon, was published in the *Aberdeen Journal* on February 28, 1849. It focuses on the parents' reactions to their child's imminent death. The first stanza describes how "for three long weary nights and days, / Above her couch in grief we hung – / Unheeded fell my words of praise, / Or lullaby her mother sung," and then readers catch a glimpse of the frail child, of her "feeble moan and deep-drawn breath, / The heavings of her little breast" (Gordon "Dying Child"). The parents' grief is felt in the lines, "Ye who have sought this house of woe, / And look upon that faded flower, / Learn from the parents' hopes laid low / The anguish of the parting hour". While most of the poem discusses the parents' sorrow, and how no one is safe from death, including tiny children, the last two lines attempt to be hopeful about Heaven, although rather unsuccessfully, due to the intense sadness of the rest of the piece. The last two lines describe how the child's soul, "ere daylight breaks will reach the skies, / And smile upon the light of Heaven". This poem, more than "The Dying Boy" mentioned in this chapter, shows how while people might want to believe in Heaven when their child dies, it is still very difficult to accept such a blow.

Scottish newspaper articles from the nineteenth century were more realistic and accepting of the finality and reality of death, more so than the poetry of the time, which tried to look at it as a positive experience, and one not to be dreaded. Such a view seems more dated now than the unsentimental accounts in the press.

Conclusion

In the nineteenth century in Scotland, child death affected everyone, no matter what social class they came from, or what geographical distances divided them. Although I have been able to uncover only a fraction of the material I wanted to, it is clear to me that child death in Scotland was seen in multiple ways. Scottish folktales often viewed child death as a form of transformation, and many child protagonists inflicted death or pain on others, in order to gain rewards. Folktales about changelings focused on the story, not on the harm done to the changeling or mistreated child.

In contrast, Scottish newspaper reports of the time depicted child death in a matter-of-fact way, giving their readers the sometimes-brutal facts, without resorting to sentimentality, and this contributed to the modern way of viewing child death – as an ending, a finality that cannot be undone. Nineteenth-century writers like MacDonald tried to comfort their readers, as well as themselves, if they, like MacDonald, had known death and sorrow in their families, by writing about death as a good experience, a new adventure, that one ought not be afraid of. Poems in nineteenth-century Scottish newspapers, such as the *Caledonian Mercury* and the *Aberdeen Journal*, also took MacDonald's view of child death. Both approaches to representing child death are equally valid, and would have provided Scottish people with a balanced view.

The issue of how child death in Scotland, during the nineteenth century, was reacted to, and represented, has raised some complicated and intriguing questions, as few scholars to date have examined the topic. There has been much work done on the subject for England, especially by Gillian Avery and Kimberley Reynolds, but even when Scottish sources are used, or referenced, they are only there to back up theories about child death in England, or Britain in general. While various librarians and archivists informed me of the difficulty of the topic, and even tried to get me to research something else, I realized how much potential scholarship could be done, for academic dissertations, or multiple books, using archival documents and library sources. I was only able to use a few of the novels and letters of George MacDonald – as he wrote sermons, letters, poems in Gaelic as well as in English, and other books that focus on Scotland, it is clear that multiple dissertations, or multiple books, could be written on the topic of child death, using just MacDonald's works for source material.

Similarly, I was lucky to stumble upon Marjory Fleming's journal – if she is an example of a Scottish child diarist who discussed death in her journals, there might be many more examples of children or adults who approached the topic in their letters, diaries and reports, and who have not been studied yet. The research just has to be done, and not brushed aside because of the difficulties, or the possible similarities to English sources. There could also be more work done in statistics and medical history. Perhaps in future years, someone will take on the challenge.

In the meantime, I hope that every person will be gentle and compassionate with others, especially regarding the sensitive topic of child death. None of us know what other people are struggling with, and death affects us all.

I hope that any readers who were kind enough to read to the end of this short book will feel free to review it, either on Amazon, Goodreads, a blog, Facebook, Instagram, BookTok, or other social media. Please feel free to reach out to me via social media:

Kayden Abley, Author (Facebook)

Kayden Abley (Goodreads)

timeskippress@gmail.com (E-mail)

Yours,

Kayden Abley

.

WORKS CITED

Primary Sources:

Barrie, J. M. *Peter Pan and Other Plays*. Oxford: Oxford University Press, 1995. Print.

Campbell, Lord Archibald. *Waifs and Strays of Celtic Tradition: Argyllshire Series*. Vol. 1. London: D. Nutt, 1889. Print.

Chambers, Robert. *Popular Rhymes of Scotland*. 1890 edition. Edinburgh: W. & R. Chambers, Ltd. 1826. Print.

"Death of His Most Excellent Majesty." *Caledonian Mercury*. 9 Feb 1820. *Nineteenth Century British Library Newspapers*. Web. 14 Aug. 2011.

"Extraordinary Case of Gross Superstition." *Caledonian Mercury*. 20 April 1840. Nineteenth Century British Library Newspapers. Web. 14 Aug. 2011.

"Glasgow Circuit Court." *Caledonian Mercury*. 30 S ep.837. *Nineteenth Century British Library Newspapers*. Web. 14 Aug. 2011.

Gordon, A. "Dying Child." *Aberdeen Journal*. 28 Fe b.1849. *Nineteenth Century British Library Newspapers*. Web. 14 Aug. 2011.

Grierson, Elizabeth. "The Milk-white Doo." *Scottish Folk and Fairy Tales*. Ed. Gordon Jarvie. Harmondsworth: Penguin Books, 1997. 9-14. Print.

Headstone: Agnes Muschett. 9 July 1813. Greyfriars Kirk. Greyfriars Place, Edinburgh, Scotland. 23 July 2011.

Hogg, James. "Adam Bell." *Scottish Folk and Fairy Tales*. Ed. Gordon Jarvie. Harmondsworth: Penguin Books, 1997. 125-131. Print.

J., K. "Dying Boy." *Aberdeen Journal*. 9 Feb.1842 . *Nineteenth Century British Library Newspapers*. Web. 14 Aug. 2011.

"Jedburgh Circuit Court." *Caledonian Mercury*.28 Sep. 1848. *Nineteenth Century British Library Newspapers*. Web. 14 Aug. 2011.

Ker Wilson, Barbara. *Scottish Folk-Tales and Legends*. London: Oxford University Press, 1954. Print.

Macbean, L. *The Story of Pet Marjorie: Together with her Journals and Letters*. London: Simpkin, Marshall, Hamilton, Kent & Co., Ltd., 1909. Print.

MacDonald, George. *The George MacDonald Treasury: The Princess and the Goblin, The Princess and Curdie, The Light Princess, Phantastes, The Giant's Heart, At the Back of the North Wind, The Golden Key, Lilith*. Ed. Glenn Kahley. Milton Keynes, U.K.: Kahley House Publishing, 2006. Print.

MacDougall, James. *Folk Tales and Fairy Lore in Gaelic and English*. Ed. George Calder. Edinburgh: John Grant, 1910. Print.

Martin, Andrew. *Scottish Endings: Writings on Death*. *Edinburgh*: National Museums of Scotland, 1996. Print.

Nic Leodhas, Sorche. *Thistle and Thyme: Tales and Legends from Scotland*. London: The Bodley Head, 1965. Print.

Secondary Sources:

Avery, Gillian. "Intimations of Mortality: The Puritan and Evangelical Message to Children." *Representations of Childhood Death*. Ed. Gillian Avery and Kimberley R Reynolds. London: MacMillan Press Ltd., 2000. 87-110.

Avery, Gillian and Kimberley Reynolds, eds. "Introduction." *Representations of Childhood Death*. London: MacMillan Press Ltd., 2000. 1-10. Print.

Gittings, Clare. "Expressions of Loss in Early Seventeenth-Century England." *The Changing Face of Death: Historical Accounts of Death and Disposal*. Ed. Peter C. Jupp and Glennys Howarth. London: MacMillian Press Ltd., 1997. 19-33. Print.

—-. "Researching People's Responses to Childhood Death in Scotland." Message to Kate Abley. 22 May 2011. E-mail.

Gordon, Anne. *Death Is for the Living*. Edinburgh: Paul Harris Publishing, 1984. Print.

Gorer, Geoffrey. *Death, Grief and Mourning in Contemporary Britain*. London: The Cresset Press, 1965. Print.

Litten, Julian. "The Funeral Trade in Hanoverian England 1714-1760." *The Changing Face of Death: Historical Accounts of Death and Disposal*. Ed. Peter C. Jupp and Glennys Howarth. London: MacMillian Press Ltd., 1997. 48-61. Print.

Loudon, Irvine. *Death in Childbirth: An International Study of Maternal Care and Maternal Mortality 1800-1950*. Oxford: Clarendon Press, 1992. Print.

Palmer, K. "Punkies." *Folklore* 83.3 (1972): 240-244. Web. 12 Aug. 2011.

Raeper, William. *George MacDonald*. Tring, Herts, England: Lion Publishing PLC, 1987. Print.

Reynolds, Kimberley. "Fatal Fantasies: The Death of Children in Victorian and Edwardian Fantasy Writing." *Representations of Childhood Death*. Ed. Gillian Avery and Kimberley Reynolds. London: MacMillan Press Ltd., 2000. 169- 188. Print.

Robb, David S. *George MacDonald*. Edinburgh: Scottish Academic Press Ltd., 1987. Print.

Simpson, Jacqueline. "The Folklore of Infant Deaths: Burials, Ghosts and Changelings." Representations of Childhood Death. Ed. Gillian Avery and Kimberley Reynolds. London: MacMillan Press Ltd., 2000. 11-28. Print.

Strange, Julie-Marie. *Death, Grief and Poverty in Britain, 1870-1914*.

Cambridge: Cambridge University Press, 2005. Print.

ABOUT THE AUTHOR

Kayden Abley is a Canadian/British author who has been published in the anthologies *Amanda Goes to Italy* (Girls Gone by Press) and *Under the Poet Tree* (Pedlar Press).

He has a diploma in Fine Arts from Dawson College, an Honors B.A. in Celtic Studies from the University of Toronto and an MSc. in Scottish Studies from the University of Edinburgh.

He also completed the academic portion of Humber College's Funeral Services Education program, where he studied grief counselling, funeral law, embalming, and funeral planning. While in the program, he assisted in performing three embalmings for funeral homes, as well as working in funeral homes in two Canadian cities, Toronto and Montreal, striving to help people who had lost loved ones.

His second full-length book, *Nonmonogamy and Death*, will be published by Thornapple Press in March 2024.